Donated
To The Library by

Delfina Ramirez

Spring 2005

Bob Mathias

Across the Fields of Gold

TRIBUTE TO AN AMERICAN HERO

By Chris Terrence
Foreword by Dick Schaap
Introduction by Bob Mathias

Bob Snodgrass
Publisher

Nelson Elliott
Managing Editor

Laura Bolter
Art Direction/Design

Michelle Washington
Publicity

Development assistance: Lois Heathman, Sharon Snodgrass, An Beard

Published by Addax Publishing Group, Inc.
Copyright © 2000 Chris Terrence

ISBN: 1-886110-90-5

Printed in the U.S.A.

1 3 5 7 9 10 8 6 4 2

ATTENTION: SCHOOLS AND BUSINESS
Addax Publishing Group, Inc. books are available at quantity discounts with
bulk purchase for education, business, or sales promotional use.
For information, please write to:
Special Sales Department,
Addax Publishing Group,
8643 Hauser Drive, Suite 235,
Lenexa, KS 66215

Library of Congress Cataloging-in-Publication Data

Terrence, Chris, 1944-
Bob Mathias : across the fields of gold : tribute to an American hero / by
Chris Terrence ; introduction by Bob Mathias ; foreword by Dick Schaap.
p. cm.
ISBN 1-886110-90-5
Mathias, Bob, 1930- 2. Athletes—United States—Biography. I. Title.

GV697.M3 T47 2000
796.42'092—dc21
[B]

00-022766

ACKNOWLEDGEMENTS

"The most important thing in the Olympic Games is not to win, but to take part, just as the most important thing in life is not the triumph, but the struggle. The essential thing is not to have conquered, but to have fought well."

-*The Olympic Creed*

What a wonderful experience this book has been for me. I could use many sports analogies to describe my feelings pertaining to this experience but the Olympic Creed pretty much captures the spirit of the adventure. There are many to thank for the help I received along the way.

First of all I would like to thank God for leading me to this story. It would be impossible to thank everyone who had an influence on this project, but the following certainly helped to make it happen: the always hard working and talented Randy Priester, Elida Jauregui for her many efforts, Dick Schaap for the beautiful foreword and the staff at the Tulare Historical Society & Museum.

Thanks so much to Nelson Elliott for bringing his great editing to this book and to Bob Snodgrass for believing in it and making it a reality through Addax. Thank you to Earl Smitcamp, Joe and Sharon Levy, John Harris, Scot Hillman, Fred Clark, Pat Tobin, Bob Jennings, Gayle Kirchner, Jim Bowman, Sue Shannon and you other great folks of the San Joaquin Valley. Thanks to the many people who told me about Bob Mathias — their brother, friend, teammate, competitor, neighbor, congressman, or those who knew him only from what he has done in life. Thanks to the wonderful Mathias family, Gene, Jim and Patricia. I only wish I could have met Dr. Charlie and Lillian.

I especially want to thank Bob and Gwen Mathias for being so gracious and helpful throughout.

C.T.

DEDICATION

For

Bill & Betty

Brad, Mary Liz, Elise, Bruce, Kathy, Phillip

Arley, Bill and Corina

Thomas

and

Paige

Terrence

Even his name sounds like something out of Greek mythology: Mathias.

He would've been at home on Mount Olympus with the rest of the gods. Zeus threw thunderbolts? Mathias threw javelins. Hermes could fly? So could Mathias. He would have fit in, too, with the legendary athletes of ancient Greece: Milo of Croton, the wrestler who was so steady he could stand on an oiled disc and brush away attackers without ever losing his footing; and Poulydamas of Thessaly, the boxer who was so brave and strong he once killed a lion with his bare hands on Mount Olympus.

Mathias of Tulare.

Robert Bruce Mathias of Tulare, a small California town in the San Joaquin Valley.

He was the stuff that myths are made on.

When he was 17, in 1948, he won the Olympic decathlon championship, the classic test of athletic skill, versatility and maturity. He had competed in his first decathlon less than two months before the Games.

When he turned 21, he ran ninety-six yards for a touchdown against Southern California and helped lift his school, Stanford, into the Rose Bowl.

In 1952, he became the first man to win the gold medal in the decathlon in two consecutive Olympics. He set a world record, won by the largest margin in Olympic history and in nine of the 10 events ran faster, jumped higher and threw farther than the first modern Olympic decathlon champion from America, the fabled Jim Thorpe.

Mathias was awarded the 1948 James E. Sullivan Award, presented annually to "the amateur athlete who, by performance, example, and good influence, did the most to advance the cause of good sportsmanship during the year."

Understandably, Hollywood decided to make a movie called *The Bob Mathias Story*. Surprisingly, Hollywood decided that the right person to play the title role was Bob Mathias. He also appeared in four other films.

After the Olympics and the movies, Mathias, unlike an earlier Olympian named Alexander the Great, still had more worlds to conquer. He moved into politics and was elected to the U.S. Congress, a member of the House of Representatives for four terms. Since then, he has traveled the world, representing the U.S. Olympic Committee, the U.S. government and countless corporations.

Bob Mathias' achievements are almost too good, and too varied, to be true. But he is neither a myth nor a god. For over half a century, Bob Mathias has been the All-American man, the essence of multitalented, a decathlete on the field and, more important, a decathlete in life.

Dick Schaap, ABC-TV/ESPN sports commentator
New York City

INTRODUCTION

When I look back over my life, I can only feel grateful for many of the things that happened to me over the years. Just like most lives, mine has been one of some ups and downs, but mostly ups in that I have always looked at myself as a pretty happy and fortunate guy. Right off the bat, I was lucky enough to be born to a loving family in Tulare, California, a small rural community in the farmlands of central California. Growing up was a terrific time, shared with my mom and dad, my brothers Gene and Jim, my sister Pat and a lot of good friends. There was no TV in those days and that, it appears, was a great blessing in itself. Us kids had to make our own fun. We'd hike, fish, play all kinds of sports and always could find things to do. When I had a bout with anemia, my family and friends helped get me through, including me in whatever activity was going on.

I had many interests growing up, but nothing more than sports. At Tulare High School, I was on the football, basketball and track teams all four years. I think I was a fairly average American high school athlete. I had a great desire to play and compete.

In my junior year at Tulare High, we came to school to learn that we had a new football coach by the name of Virgil Jackson. Little did I know what a profound effect Coach Jackson would have on my life. He was an excellent coach and led us to conference championships in football and track. He taught us how to win through good work ethics, believing in ourselves and the power of good teamwork. In track, he studied hard on all the various events and worked with us individually. In his research, Virgil had read about the decathlon event, which featured athletes competing in ten different track events over a two-day period. He also found that there was a decathlon meet, the Pasadena Games, in June, coming up at the Los Angeles Coliseum, just after my graduation from Tulare High in 1948. Coach came to me about the idea of going out for the meet and said that he thought it would be a great experience for me to try because I had done pretty well in four of the events of the decathlon and that he thought it might be fun for me to try the other six and enter the meet. I jumped at the opportunity, thinking it would be fun to get to be in another track meet that year. Coach Jackson, along with my family members and friends, helped me train and prepare for the meet.

Virgil Jackson was a truly outstanding coach. He wasn't like some famous coaches that you hear about, that get great high school athletes in college. Coach Jackson TAUGHT us in high school and set us on a path and we did O.K. because he showed us how to do this and that — not just me, but many others, including Sim Innes, my high school buddy and teammate who went on to win a gold medal in the discus event in the 1952 Olympics. Many other teammates from our days in Tulare went on to successes in college sports or better yet, in life in general.

When Chris Terrence approached me with the idea of doing this book, I thought of it as a great way to thank so many of the people that have been a help in my life. Just thumbing through the manuscript brings back a lot of memories. I think Chris has done a great job capturing "the feeling" of the time all the things that happened in my life. I only wish all the friends who helped me could be mentioned, but, alas, that would take a very, very thick book.

Thank you and God Bless,

BOB MATHIAS

Across the Fields of Gold

"There was always this - something - about Robert. It amazed me. He was precious. I remember as a kid, he could get on that action bar, turn flips, and walk on his hands, just naturally! Even as a baby, he could fall out of the highchair and land on his feet!"

Dr. Eugene Mathias, talking about his famous brother.

Robert Bruce Mathias was born to Dr. Charlie and Lillian, on November 17, 1930. He was the second of the four Mathias children — Eugene, Robert, James and Patricia, all three years apart in age.

Bob had a bout with anemia, but didn't let it stop him. Jim Mathias said, "It never really manifested itself. He just went ahead. Robert was a competitor and loved to run and do as much as he could. He was very gifted and could run faster than any other kid."

Eugene told this story: "One afternoon my friend Dink Templeton and I decided to go over to Wilson Elementary School to try some jumps in the high jump pit. Bob tagged along. So the guys and I get to this certain height and we just can't get over it. Bob asked if he could try and we told him 'later.' After all, he was three years younger than us! Well, when 'later' finally came and we still couldn't get over the bar, Bob got up, walked over to the bar, got back away from it, ran in and — up and over, no sweat. Cleared it easy. My friends and I just looked at each other. That was the first time I thought there was something very special about Bob's ability."

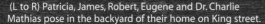

(L to R) Patricia, James, Robert, Eugene and Dr. Charlie Mathias pose in the backyard of their home on King street.

Lillian Mathias

9

"The thing I remember most about my folks is that they never 'pushed me' to do this or do that in any sport. What they did do was support me and they were always there for me, encouraging me, but letting me make my own decisions about what I was doing on the field. I've always appreciated that and I have been fortunate enough to realize how much that meant to me."

Bob Mathias

The football field and the track in the stadium on the campus of Tulare Union High School look pretty much the same as they did a half a century ago. Oh yes, there have been some changes, maybe more stands have been built, there is a new press box, and, yes, the name of the school itself was Tulare High School back then in the mid 1940s. The name of the stadium is now the Bob Mathias Stadium and it's just a short walk across the shady campus to the Sim Iness gymnasium. The facilities are named for two of Tulare's most treasured citizens in honor of some amazing glories these fellas brought to the community. Imagine one school having not one, but two members of the same class, going off, halfway around the world and winning gold medals in the Olympics!

Sim Iness was a football coach's dream. Huge, quick, with power and speed, he was the biggest lineman in the San Joaquin Valley in his senior year, tipping the scales at 247 pounds, stretched over a 6-foot 6-inch frame. People used to call him Big Sim. He weighed in at 13 pounds, 10 ounces at birth, bless his mother! Sim often joked, "I was so big that my mother won a blue ribbon at the Oklahoma State Fair. (Sim was born in Oklahoma.) She always told everyone that I was born on July 9, 10 and 11!"

Tulare High coaches Virgil Jackson and Ernie Lambrecht would be great influences on Bob and Sim in their rise to the top of the Olympic victory stand.

Mathias and Iness began to draw quite a bit of attention from track fans. Iness had to be talked into coming out for the weight events in track, as he wanted to play baseball instead. Once he got into it, he started racking up some impressive numbers in the discus and shot put events. A friendly rivalry began to brew between the two athletes, with Bob also producing some excellent distances in the same events. Bob was also outstanding in the hurdles, sprints and long jump.

Coach Virgil Jackson

Dr. Charlie
Bob
Lillian

The future champion of the world takes a moment
from one of his many backyard workouts.

Bob Mathias

Bob's high school days in Tulare were blessed with family, friends and a strong community. He was basically shy but friendly and humble, even after his football and track achievements brought him a great deal of attention. He was a typical American teenager in the late 1940s. Little did Bob, nor did anyone else, have a clue how much his world would change over the next four months, when track coach Virgil Jackson showed him what a javelin was on a sunny April afternoon on the Tulare High practice field. At this point, Bob was still two months away from entering his first decathlon

"Four months before the 1948 Olympics, Bob Mathias had never SEEN a javelin!!"

and 16 weeks away from winning the Olympic gold in England. Surely one of the greatest sports stories of all time.

"He told me that he thought I had been competing at a good level in a lot of the events that were in a decathlon and that we could work on the ones I didn't know," Bob said. Together, Virgil and Bob brought the idea to Dr. Charlie and Lillian. They thought it was interesting but left the decision up to Bob. The rest is history.

Let's quote *Ripley's Believe It Or Not!* — for what happened after that: "On November 17, 1947, Tulare High track coach Virgil Jackson, suggested to 17-year-old Bob Mathias, a hurdles and sprint star the previous spring, that he begin thinking about working on some other track events like the javelin, pole vault, high jump and distance running ... and 232 days later, young Mathias won the Olympic decathlon!! Two months before the 1948 Olympic games, Bob Mathias had not only never competed in a decathlon, he had never competed in six of the 10 events!! Four months before the 1948 Olympics, Bob Mathias had never tried the pole vault!"

Four months before the 1948 Olympics, Coach Jackson introduces Bob to the javelin.

The decathlon is a two-day miniature track meet designed to ascertain the sport's best all-around athlete. Participants compete in 10 different track and field events and are scored against an international scoring table for each event. The winner is the athlete with the highest total score. Within the rules of track and field, each athlete must sprint for 100 meters, long jump, heave a 16-pound ball, high jump and run 400 meters, all in that set order, on the first day. On the second day the athlete runs a 110-meter hurdle race over ten 42-inch barriers, hurls the discus, pole vaults, tosses a javelin, and, if not exhausted by then, races 1500 meters, about a mile.

Bob was not nervous at the Pasadena Games held at the LA Coliseum June 10 and 11. "I was just happy to be there. It was like another track meet. There was no pressure on me," Bob remembered. The meet was a qualifier for the Olympic Team trials at Bloomfield, N.J., to be held on June 28 and 29. Bob, competing in six of the events for the first time, shocked everyone by winning the event and scoring more than 7,000 points, the only athlete to do so. His final score of 7,094 was the best total in the decathlon in the world since 1940! Two weeks later, at Bloomfield, in just his second decathlon and up against some of the greatest athletes in the world, Bob upped that score to 7,224! Look out world, Bob Mathias was going to the Olympics!

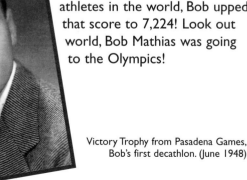

Victory Trophy from Pasadena Games, Bob's first decathlon. (June 1948)

Irving Mondschein was the national decathlon champion in 1944, 1946 and 1947. He was a track and football star at New York University. Irving had been favored to win the Olympic decathlon in 1948.

Another favored decathlete was Floyd Simmons from the University of North Carolina. Simmons also was a football star for the Tar Heels and a one-time national high school high hurdles champion in track. Floyd led after the first day in Bloomfield at the trials. He was impressed with Bob after reading about him and seeing him perform, but felt that Bob wouldn't have enough strength to win such a grueling event at such a young age, in particular in the distance events. "I learned never to underestimate Bob Mathias," Floyd Simmons said. "He was a great athlete, but oh my, what a competitor!" It was Mathias, Mondschein and Simmons who would represent the U.S.A. in the decathlon in the 1948 Olympics, in London, England.

Irving Mondschein

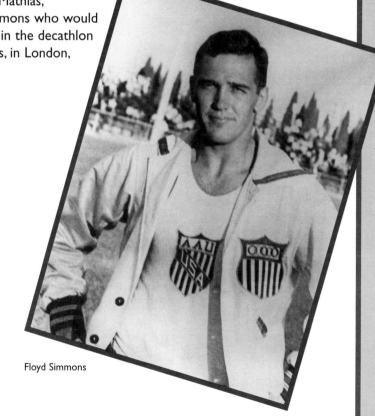

Floyd Simmons

"I learned never to underestimate Bob Mathias," Floyd Simmons said. "He was a great athlete, but oh my, what a competitor!"

1948

The U.S.A. Olympic team marches into Wembley Stadium in the summer of 1948.

"We sent a boy over to do a man's job and he did it far better than any man ever could."

Paul Helms
Founder, Helms Athletic Foundation

For a young man of 17 who had never been out of California before his trip to Bloomfield, N.J., to compete in the Olympic trials, imagine how Bob Mathias felt going over to England on the boat with the U.S. Olympic team a month later. Perhaps one of the best insights about how this extraordinary young man handled things came in the following letter he wrote to Patricia, his 11-year-old sister, while he was in England:

August 8, 1948

Dear Patricia,
I bet it's really cool up there in the mountains.
You would have liked the boat, Patricia. It was 366 feet long and had five decks on it. They had shuffle board and Ping-Pong tables to play on. They had two bands on the ship and they played at dances every night. And guess what? At dinner they had a band playing dinner music for us. They had all the food you could eat on the ship, too. The Olympics gave us a complete outfit to wear over here. We got a hat, shirt, tie, two pairs of pants, a belt and buckle, socks, and a pair of white shoes. They gave us a slip-over sweater with an Olympic design on the front. It's too small for me so when I get back, I think I'll give it to you if it fits.
The first two days on the boat I got dizzy and didn't feel very good, but after that I was all right. You would of liked the swimming pool they had on the boat. It was salt water and it hurt your eyes, but it was fun to go swimming in it. It took seven days to get over to England. Eugene got here two days ago and it only took him one day by airplane. Mother hasn't got here yet but she'll be here tonight.
I bet that it hasn't rained up in the mountains. It rained in England twice. The rest of the time, it's real windy. The last three days it's been pretty hot. Not as hot as Tulare though. I'm working real hard so I can win the Olympics. I don't know if I can or not but I will try real hard. If I win it or even get one of the three places, I'll bring you home a medal. After the Olympics are over I'm going to Paris, France, to be in another meet. Don't eat too much up there.

Love and kisses,
Robert xxxxx ooooo

At the end of the first day of competition, Bob was in third place, but not far off the pace set by the leader, Enrique Kistenmacher of Argentina, with Ignace Heinrich of France in second place. The key was that Bob felt he was in good shape because he "hadn't really made mistakes and also I hadn't competed in my good events yet." The second day a great discus throw by Bob in the second event put him in the lead to stay. He just had to stay close in the remaining events and he did in the pole vault, his weakest event, by clearing 11'6". (Remember, his first pole vault — ever — was just four months prior.) He also managed a good throw in the javelin event. Then came the realization that if he ran the 1500 meters race in under six minutes, he could win the

17-year-old Bob Mathias on the deck of the U.S.S. America as his incredible adventure unfolds. With Bob are his decathlon teammates Irving "Moon" Mondschein (left) and Floyd Simmons (front), along with Coach Ward Haylett.

In a cold, London rain Mathias easily clears 11 feet in the pole vault at Wembley Stadium.

gold medal. The delays were long and the cold and the rain made the waits very tough. Bob kept a blanket around him to try to keep warm and dry. The 1500-meter race didn't go off until close to 11 p.m. The athletes had been on the field for 12 hours and they were cold, tired and hungry. It was dark and the track was dimly lit in the dreary weather as the race began.

1500 Meters to the Gold

To cover that race, let's go to the words of loyal mom, Lillian Mathias, as she described it in Wembley Stadium after the event: "Just before the men went across the field to the start of the 1500 meters, the coaches told Bob that he could beat Heinrich by running the race under six minutes. Eugene came and told me this. I didn't think Bob could do it, he looked so tired and drawn. He appeared to be utterly exhausted. He had been out there for 12 hours and although he had a box lunch, cubes of sugar and some nutrition pills, he told me after it was over that he had never been so hungry in his life.

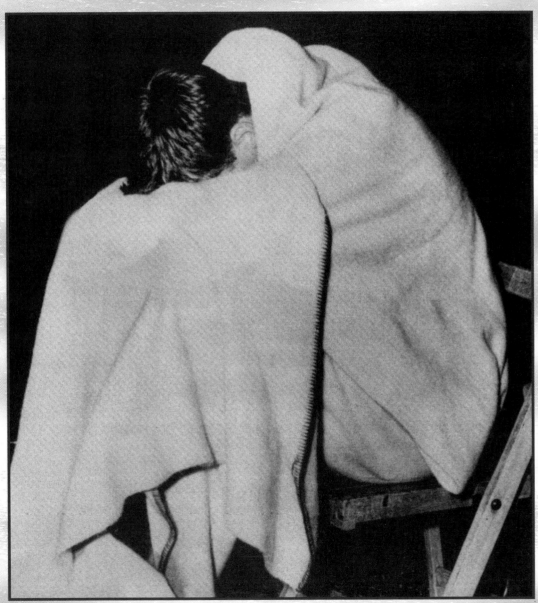

"Charlie, Jimmy and I were down as close to the track as we could get. The stands were empty, the only activity being up in the press box, on the field, and among our little group of die-hard fans. We could see the orange spurt of the flame when the gun started the runners, but the fog was so dense we could not distinguish Robert from another runner, Peter Mullins. Both wore white, satin suits. Eugene was over in the infield side of the track where he could call out the time of the laps to Robert. Andersson (of Sweden) came by us first, then Robert about 20 yards behind him and Mullins about the same distance back of Robert. Robert was trying to keep pace with the Swedish boy. Eugene yelled to him to slow down, but he didn't do it. We didn't see them again until they came around for the end of the second lap with Robert about the same distance behind Andersson. Again Eugene shouted for him to slow down, but he still didn't listen. He figured if he could stay close to the Swede, he would run the 1500 meters well under six minutes, but Eugene was afraid he would collapse and not finish at all. The third time around, Robert had definitely slowed down, not because he wanted to but because he had to. He was pretty far back of Andersson now. That was when I really thought I would die. He had one more lap to go and I really felt that he couldn't do it. He was so very tired. A small bunch of boys from Pepperdine College in Los Angeles were yelling, 'Come on, Tulare,' and it gave us all heart to know we had friends over there somewhere in the dark. Andersson came in to finish all alone. Robert was way back in the dark, somewhere on the other side of the track ... I think all of us were praying. We could only stand there and wait for him. We could not see him at all, didn't even know just how far behind he was. We had seen others fall to the track. Was that what had happened to our boy? None of us knew.

"Pretty soon, here he came. He wasn't running, just jogging. His head was down, his hands just swinging and he seemed to be watching the track.

"The boys from Pepperdine began whooping it up some more to 'Come on, Tulare!' I just stood there and bawled and prayed he would stay on his feet until he crossed the finish line. When he had about 20 meters to go, something seemed to happen to him that snapped him out of it. He threw his head back and speeded up, as if he had just suddenly realized that he was nearing the finish and was not still out there alone in the dark, miles from home. He started to run with his arms up again. He crossed the line standing up, and his father and one of the trainers ran out on to the track to catch him. They walked him up and down about ten minutes. His feet had cramped, and he was sick to his stomach. And he had won the Olympic decathlon."

(Lillian Mathias' account of the 1500-meter race, to Maxwell Stiles of Sports World.)

(cont. on p. 26)

A couple of golden moments - Bob crosses the finish line to win and gets a hug from mom.

A PROUD COACH REMEMBERS

Virgil Jackson, the Tulare High track coach who came up with the idea of Bob's entering the decathlon in the first place remembered the moment: "I was pretty excited after Bob had made the Olympic team, but I was fit to be tied that second day of the decathlon at London. I was in the office of one of our two newspapers, *The Tulare Bee*, receiving the news as fast as it came in over the teletype. When the news came through that Bob had won and everybody in town went mad, I somehow or other managed to walk out of that editorial office and down to the street. I don't know how I got there, but later I found myself alone on a park bench for 20 minutes and crying like a baby. Things like that just don't happen to a high school coach, but it just happened to me."

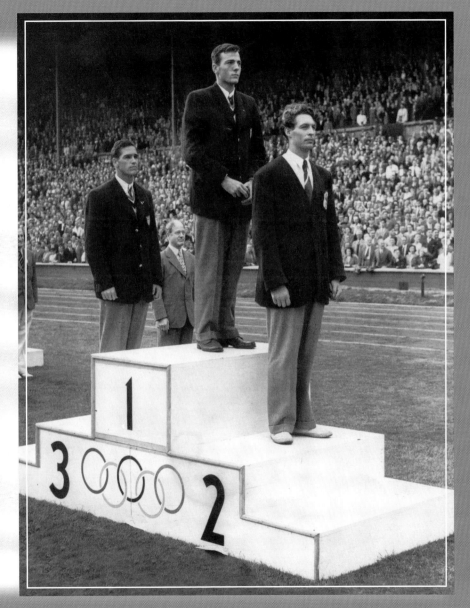

Bob Mathias (U.S.A.) gold, Ignace Heinrich (France) silver and Floyd Simmons (U.S.A.) bronze (left).

(cont. from p. 24)

It was over. Bob Mathias had won the gold medal. He'd finished with 7,139 points, 165 more than Ignace Heinrich of France and 189 points ahead of U.S.A. teammate Floyd Simmons. Bob had made history in becoming the youngest athlete in history to win an Olympic gold medal in track and field. He slept well that night. In fact, he had to be awakened the next day to catch the athlete's bus over to Wembley Stadium to take his place on the victory stand, receive his medal and hear the American national anthem played before another crowd of 80,000.

Earl Gustkey, in an article he wrote about Bob in 1987 in the *LA Times,* asked Bob what his most vivid memory of that 1948 Olympic experience was. "It's two things actually," Bob answered. "The first was the shock of seeing all the World War II bombing damage in London. I was just a kid from Tulare, who'd only heard about the war on the radio and read about it. There were still piles of rubble all over the place, and bomb craters. The second thing is the last event, the 1500 meters. By then, I knew that any decent time at all would win it for me ... Wembley was a poorly lighted place. They had dog racing there, and we were running only by the dog racing lights, 8-foot light poles about 50 feet apart, right on the infield side of the track. So I was running alone, from misty darkness into misty pools of light and back into misty darkness again. The whole situation had become unbelievable to me — I didn't think I had a chance in the world of winning when I got to London — but that 1500 made it seem really strange."

"In a cold rain, on a track covered with water ... in fading light and finally, under flood lights, it was an amazing achievement."

Allison Danzig
The New York Times

Governor Honors Bob Tonight

Bob, on the way home, stops by the White House for a visit with President Harry S. Truman.

Chief Executive to Attend Testimonial

California's chief executive tonight will help up its three-day homecoming celebration for Bob year-old Olympic decathlon champion.

Gov. Earl Warren, republican vice preside wired local celebration officials that he was "only cept your cir... take part" in t... for Mathias,

The chief e... both the te... the fairgrounds open air b... the fairgr...

his vaca... ira H to...

Fol... Alex... Cha... his...

Monday, August 30, 1948

GOVERNOR HONORS BOB MATHIAS:

Chief Executive Guest at Testimonial Dinner Here

(Continued from page 1)
will pay tribute to the athletic accomplishments of two other Tulareans, Sim Iness and Bill LaThorpe.

Iness, who will enter Compton college next week, will be honor-ed for winning the Southwest Pacific AAU discus champion

opened with Mayor Elmo R. Zumwalt delivering the city's official greetings. Dr. and Mrs. Charles Mathias, the champ's parents; Champion Bob and Gov. Warren will deliver short talks to the dinner crowd.

Swinging out to the grand-stand, Mayor Zumwalt will re-peat his official greetings.

Following the greetings, Ma-thias, Iness and LaThorpe will be introduced to the throng and will speak briefly.

Scheduled to speak during the ... ceremonies are Ea... layed with ... at ...

Mathias to be Nominated for Sullivan Award

Bob Mathias, Tulare's 17-year old Olympic decathlon champion recommended for the ... trophy. No ...

WELCOME BOBBY

OLYMPIC DECATHLON Champion

Welcome Home Bob

WESTERN UNION
(THE WESTERN UNION TELEGRAPH COMPANY)
CABLEGRAM
CANADIAN NATIONAL TELEGRAPHS.

ANGLO-AMERICAN TELEGRAPH CO. LD. 7, OLD BOND STREET, LONDON, W.1. (Tel. No. Regen' 01... 7 N 6 3

RECEIVED AT 7, OLD BOND STREET, LONDON, W.1.

OB 512 THE WHITE HOUSE WASHINGTON DC 55 7 1208P =

ROBERT MATHIAS =

OLYMPIC HEADQUARTERS =WEMBLY STADIUM WEMBLEY =

37 UPPER BROOK ST W1-

=BY WINNING THE OLYMPIC DECATHLON CHAMPIONSHIP YOU HAVE DEMONSTRATED ABUNDANTLY THAT THE GLORY OF AMERICA IS ITS YOUTH. IN THE NAME OF THE NATION TO WHICH YOU HAVE BROUGHT SUCH OUTSTANDING DISTINCTION I EXTEND HEARTY CONGRATULATIONS

ALL OF YOUR FELLOW AMERICANS ARE PROUD OF YOU=

HARRY S TRUMAN

Please send your Reply "Via WESTERN UNION" You may telephone us for a messenger

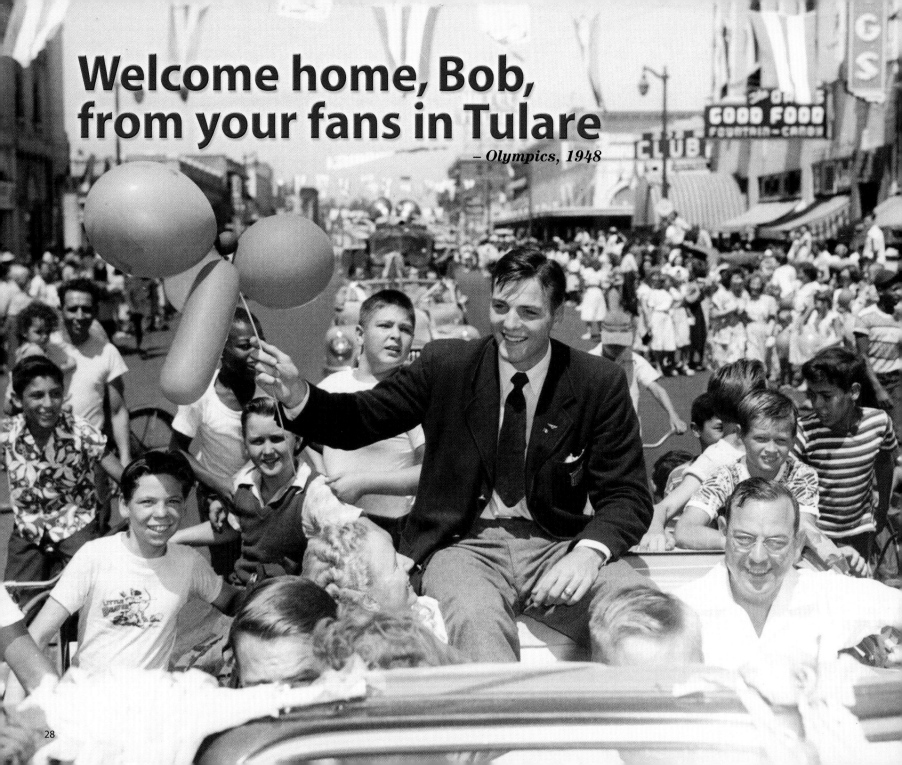

Welcome home, Bob, from your fans in Tulare
– Olympics, 1948

(far right) The Sullivan Award, honoring America's top amateur athlete, went to Bob Mathias in 1948.

(right) Bob checks out *Life* magazine story with Glenn Mathias Jackson, son of Virgil and Fritzie Jackson.

The legends get together. Jim Thorpe and Bob Mathias meet in Los Angeles in December of 1948.

OLYMPIC DECATHLON
Champion

Welcome Home Bob

A MATHIAS MEMORY

My first recollection of Bob Mathias was when I saw him in *The Movietone News* at the Rivoli Theatre on Main Street in Hempstead, New York, around 1956. I was a twelve-year-old sports nut at the time and very much a fan of Mickey Mantle and the Yankees, Frank Gifford and the Giants, Sweetwater Clifton and the Knicks and Notre Dame football. Sports were big at our house. One day, I had seen a story at the Rivoli about how this young athlete from California had won the Olympic gold medal in the decathlon at a very young age, then won it again four years later in 1952, and then wasn't allowed to participate in the 1956 Games for a reason I didn't understand too well. (I still don't!) *The Movietone News* story (remember them?) showed this talented and handsome hero traveling around the world as an ambassador of sorts, promoting the 1956 Olympics and working with other American athletes in preparation for the competition even though he wasn't going to be in the Games as a participant that year. My dad told me that it was a good indication of what kind of man Bob Mathias was — that he would help his teammates even though he was ineligible to compete. Through the years, I would remember Bob Mathias and that story. To this day, I am still completely amazed how a 17-year-old youngster could win the Olympic gold medal in the decathlon. It has to be one of the greatest accomplishments in the history of sports.

Bob won his first Olympics in the dark. Wembley Stadium was shrouded in a dense fog, so much so that what few spectators were there had difficulty telling the competitors apart. Bob's parents of course, were there at the end, for the final event, the 1500 meters. Lillian, Bob's mother, feared that Bob was at a state of near exhaustion. The coaches told Bob he could win the gold medal if he just ran under six minutes, a really slow time. But at that moment, it seemed a tall order. With Mom and Dad alternately praying and crying, and a small group of guys from southern California yelling, "Come on, Tulare," Bob started the race. He trudged on. And on. He was sick to his stomach. He was cramping. With the finish in sight, he picked up his pace. He crossed the line, and needed help to walk. He was spent. He had given everything. And he was an Olympic champion.

In the early '90s I was lucky enough to have my own television talk show in Fresno, California, *On Tonight! With Chris Terrence*. The show was on five nights a week and featured many local guests as well as more famous folks from the worlds of entertainment, the arts, the political world, and athletes of all kinds. I was very excited to learn one day that Bob Mathias was booked to be on the show. Living in central California, I had come to hear a lot more about Bob Mathias. Besides his Olympic triumphs, his acting career, his four terms as a congressman in the U.S. House of Representatives, I heard other stories about Bob Mathias the person. Stories about what a great guy he is, and despite the fame and glory and all that he accomplished, very approachable. When I met him, I found the stories were true. Right away it felt like I had known him a long time. As time went on, Bob was gracious enough to come back for visits on the show and we developed a friendship. He invited me to some events on his land in Kings Canyon where he built and ran the Bob Mathias Olympic Camp for Boys and Girls. Getting to know this American legend was indeed a pleasure. Bob and his wife Gwen often hosted campouts and fish fries for their many friends from Tulare, Stanford University, and, literally, from all over the world. I have often marveled at how this guy who had accomplished so much in his life was still just a regular guy and an unassuming friend to all. During my association with Bob, I have met his family, hometown friends, many of his college buddies, teammates and famous and not-so-famous people who love him.

I am proud to call him my friend.

C.T.

KISKI PREP

When Bob Mathias came back to Tulare after his great Olympic triumph, he soon had to embark on another journey. He had been recruited by Stanford University and had decided to go there. There was good news and bad news. The good news was that he wanted to go to Stanford and prepare to become a doctor like his father before him. Also because his brother Eugene was attending Stanford, in pre-Med. The bad news was that he had to bring up an English grade as an entrance requirement. Stanford suggested that Bob attend Kiski Prep School in Saltsburg, Pennsylvania, to get the famous young athlete ready for the rigors of the Stanford curriculum. Bob Hoegh, a high school buddy of Mathias, and a teammate in football and track at Tulare High, was offered the same type scholarship to Stanford, and also needed some grade repairs on his transcript. The two friends traveled cross country to Kiski for a year of prep school. It turned out to be a great year for both Bobs as they did well in their academics and also in sports (football and track). Mathias served as class secretary in student government, was a member of the Library Club and was also in the Glee Club. At the Kiski commencement ceremonies in June, Bob Mathias won an award for having done the most for the school. Bob Hoegh won the Citizenship award. Both went on to stellar careers at Stanford.

"Bob was the boy who came here great and left greater."

Kiski Prep yearbook, 1949

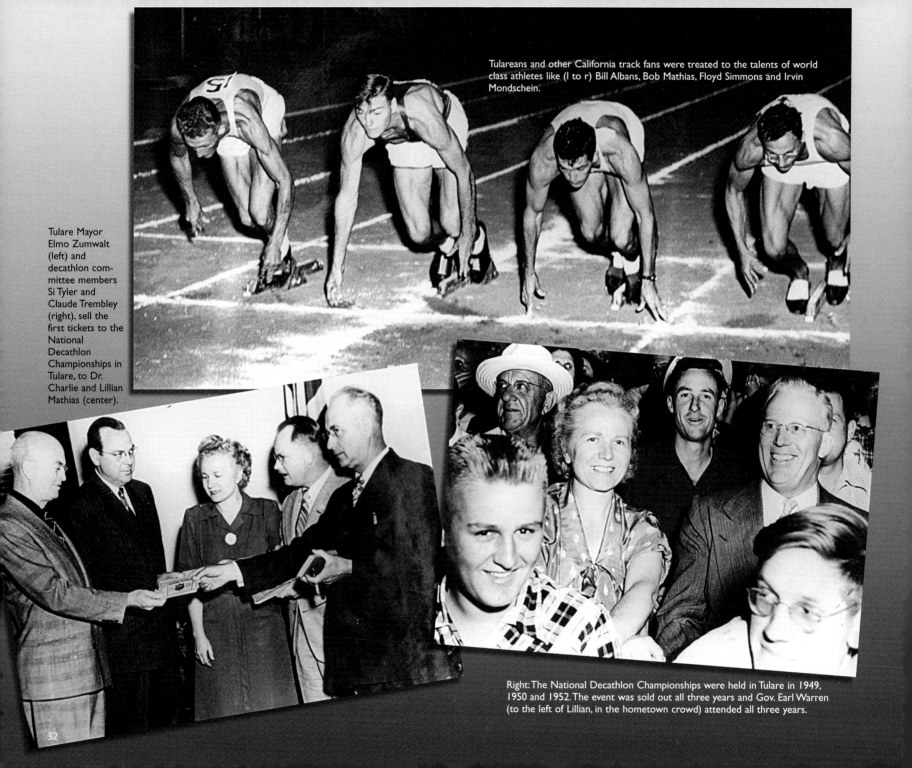

Tulareans and other California track fans were treated to the talents of world class athletes like (l to r) Bill Albans, Bob Mathias, Floyd Simmons and Irvin Mondschein.

Tulare Mayor Elmo Zumwalt (left) and decathlon committee members Si Tyler and Claude Trembley (right), sell the first tickets to the National Decathlon Championships in Tulare, to Dr. Charlie and Lillian Mathias (center).

Right: The National Decathlon Championships were held in Tulare in 1949, 1950 and 1952. The event was sold out all three years and Gov. Earl Warren (to the left of Lillian, in the hometown crowd) attended all three years.

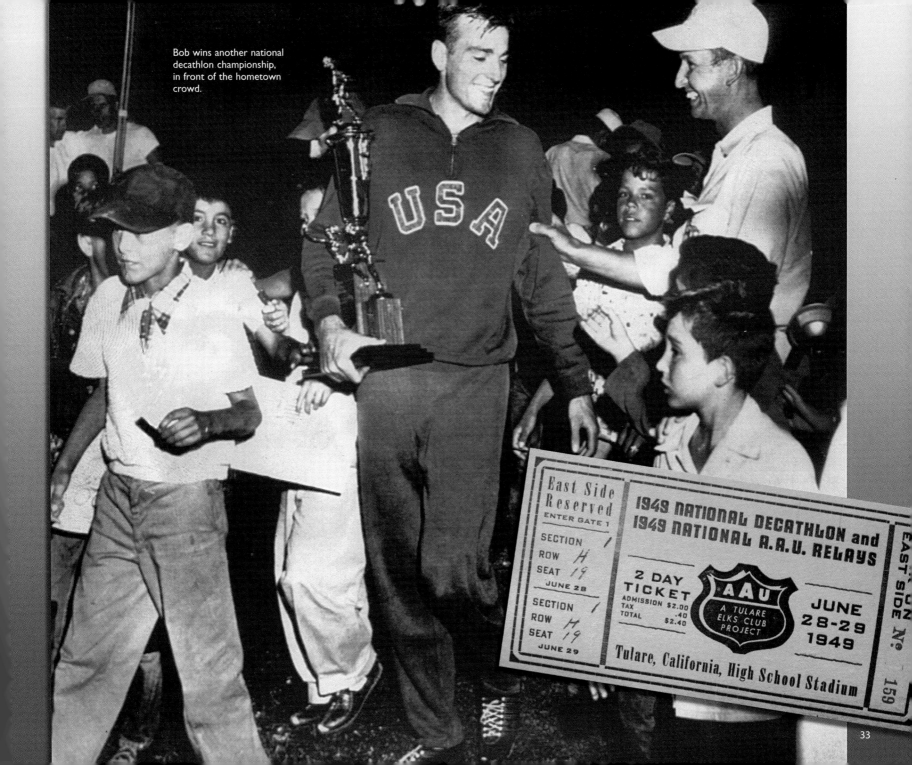

Bob wins another national decathlon championship, in front of the hometown crowd.

East Side Reserved
ENTER GATE 1

SECTION 1
ROW H
SEAT 19
JUNE 28

SECTION 1
ROW H
SEAT 19
JUNE 29

1949 NATIONAL DECATHLON and
1949 NATIONAL A.A.U. RELAYS

2 DAY TICKET
ADMISSION $2.00
TAX .40
TOTAL $2.40

AAU
A TULARE
ELKS CLUB
PROJECT

JUNE 28-29 1949

Tulare, California, High School Stadium

EAST SIDE No. 159

In the four years that Bob attended Stanford he was a busy man. He led the Indians' track teams for three years and also would play varsity football for two years. Bob was a hard working student, earning a Bachelor of Arts degree in education and also was a member of the Platoon Leadership Class, becoming an officer in the U.S. Marines after his June, 1953, graduation from Stanford. Bob was a member of the Phi Gamma Delta fraternity, where he met some "of the greatest friends you could ever ask for. We still get together as often as possible today and it is always a terrific time," Bob remembers. It amazed many how well Bob was able to concentrate on his studies, with all the distractions, but he did. In track at the school, he was named an All-American all three years.

In 1951, Stanford head football coach Chuck Taylor received a nice surprise. Bob Mathias, the "world's best all-around athlete," came out for football. It would not be easy for the one-time Tulare High running back. He had not played in three years and did not attend any spring workouts where the offense is taught, plus Mathias had to work his way into some playing time with three good letterman in front of him on the player depth chart. To make matters worse, Bob had to play through some early season injuries. He didn't even make the travel squad for the first two games of the year. He did make the trip to Ann Arbor, Michigan, for the third game of the 1951 campaign, in which he got minor playing time. But the next week, against UCLA, starting fullback Bob Meyers was hurt and Bob was put in the lineup for the Indians. Being the incredible competitor that he is, Mathias answered the bell against the always tough Bruins, scoring two touchdowns and helping to put Stanford in the eye of Pacific Coast Conference fans. The 21-7 victory against UCLA showed that Stanford had to be considered as a possible contender for the Rose Bowl. The Indians had won four straight.

Bob puts the shot for the Stanford team. He was named All-American in track for three years.

"What USC - Stanford Game?"

The undefeated records by the two schools along with that coveted Rose Bowl berth hanging in the balance built an incredible momentum for what would be the big showdown — USC vs. Stanford, for all the marbles. More than 100,000 rabid football fans showed up at the Los Angeles Coliseum to watch the battle.

Two views of Bob's 96-yard kickoff return for a touchdown as over 100,000 look on at the L.A. Coliseum. This play led Stanford to a come-from-behind victory against USC and into the Rose Bowl.

It was a game that is still thought of as one of college football's greatest games. Bob Mathias and USC's Frank Gifford, longtime friends still have some laughs about it today (although Gifford probably just a couple less than Mathias!). "If I haven't seen Frank in a while, I always like to say to him, 'Hey Frank, remember that USC-Stanford game in '51?'"

"What USC-Stanford game?" is Gifford's usual, good-natured reply.

The 27-20 victory over USC in 1951 was the highlight of the year for the Stanford football team. They were plagued with injuries in the final games of the season and lost in the Rose Bowl to Illinois 40-7. Both Bob Mathias and Frank Gifford would later be selected in the National Football League draft. Gifford went on to star with the New York Giants while Bob continued his decathlon career and started a family. In those days, the NFL was still in its early stages and the salaries certainly were not the way they are today. Bob has expressed regret that he didn't play pro football but obviously went on to success across other fields. Stanford football coach Chuck Taylor said of Bob, "Bob could have been at least as great a football player as he was a decathlete. That is fact. For as great as he played, while his time to play was cut short because of his track commitments, well, it was just amazing."

Above: Mathias scores his second touchdown of the fourth quarter as Stanford keeps coming back against USC.

TIME

THE WEEKLY NEWSMAGAZINE

TWENTY CENTS

JULY 21, 1952

BOB MATHIAS
In the 1952 Olympics, 69 nations and a one-man track team.

$6.00 A YEAR

VOL. LX NO. 3

In July of 1952, on the cover of *TIME* magazine, there was a portrait of the reigning Olympic decathlon champion, superimposed over the stadium site of the upcoming Olympic Games in Helsinki, Finland. The caption under the artwork on the face of the famous magazine read: "Bob Mathias — In the 1952 Olympics, 69 nations and a one-man track team." What a perfect way to describe the situation 21-year-old Bob Mathias found himself in while getting ready for his second Olympics.

1952

Harrison Dillard,
Bob and Mal
Whitfield, winners
of gold in 1948,
look for more in
1952.

Bob and fellow decathlete Floyd
Simmons visit with Japanese athletes
at the Olympic Village in Helsinki.

"The second Olympics were a lot more fun for me than the first," Bob remembered. **"I knew more about the events. I was more confident. I'd get down in the blocks and knew I was going to tear through those things. The feeling was so good. Everything just clicked for two days."**

Despite a muscle injury he received in the long jump, the second event of the first day, Bob was brilliant. "The muscle pull did scare me a bit but it wasn't a major injury. The trainer put a wrap on it and I was able to continue," Bob remembered. He continued indeed, besting every time and length of his gold medal-winning performance in London. He took first in five of the 10 events (shot put, 400 meters, discus, pole vault and javelin), and became the first man in history to win the Olympic decathlon gold twice. He finished 912 points ahead of second-place finisher Milt Campbell. Floyd Simmons again won the bronze to complete the American sweep in the event.

Bob's points total in Helsinki, 7,887, was a new world record. Matching his performance, event for event, man for man, Bob would have defeated the legendary Jim Thorpe, the hero of the 1912 Olympics, by more than 1600 points!

Injured leg and all, Bob throws the javelin 194 feet, 3 1/8 inches en route to the decathlon gold medal and world record.

Bob goes 22 feet and 10 3/4 inches in the long jump but pulls a leg muscle in doing so. It was only the second event of the first day. Bob would have to work through the pain to win.

Another thrill for Bob, and for the homefolks back in Tulare, was that this time, high school teammate and good buddy, Sim Iness, had not only made the U.S.A. Olympic squad, but also won the gold medal in the discus with an Olympic record heave of 180 feet, 6.85 inches. Sim had made the squad by winning the U.S.A. trials despite a heavily bandaged, swollen knee.

A tired Bob Mathias crosses familiar ground. The finish of the 1500 meters to claim his second gold medal (setting a new world record).

Tom Hennion charts the progress of Bob and Sim on the tote board in the Tulare Hotel. Fans pack the lobby to keep current on the dynamic duo across the world in Helsinki, Finland.

Sim and Bob were greeted back home with open arms. There were parades and special events all over the Valley for the winners of the Olympic gold.

After the '52 Games, Bob performed in meets in Oslo, Norway, Glasgow, Scotland, Cologne, West Berlin and Dortmund in Germany, Zurich, Switzerland, and Boraas, Sweden. It had been quite a year for this young man.

HOLLYWOOD COMES A CALLIN'

1954

Besides everything else, he became the only man ever to play in the Rose Bowl and win a gold medal in the Olympics in the same year. How do you follow a year like that? Well, how about with a Hollywood movie on your life?

Many times, probably because decathletes are considered the best all-around athletes in the world, the champions of the lot are oftentimes invited to Hollywood to be in the movies. When Allied Artists decided to do a movie on the life of Bob Mathias, they took a good look at who would be the best to play Bob. They were looking for someone with matinee idol good looks, someone bright, enthusiastic, and, of course, it would really help if he was a good athlete. Seems logical that they came up with who they did: Bob Mathias. The film starred Bob, Ward Bond, Ann Doran and Howard Petrie.

Bob signs his first movie contract in 1954. He will star in *The Bob Mathias Story*.

Above: Bob gets set to play Bob.

THE BOB MATHIAS STORY

In the last scene of *The Bob Mathias Story*, you see Bob, in his U.S. Marine Corps uniform, saluting the flag. Well, that's where the movie left off and that's where Bob's active duty tour in the Marines began. Soon after the filming was done, Bob was in Quantico, Virginia, for six months basic training in the Marines. He was then stationed at Camp Pendelton, in San Diego, for two years. While there, Bob was part of the Marines' UDT (Underwater Demolition Team).

From left to right below:

Bob wasn't the only local Tularean to get a part in *The Bob Mathias Story*. Some of the scenes were shot on location in Tulare and locals were used as extras.

Coach Jackson, meet Coach Jackson. (That's Ward Bond on the right.)

The Mathias's meet themselves. That is Dr. Charlie and Lillian flanked by Ann Doran and Howard Petrie. The real parents meet the reel parents.

Ward Bond looks on as Bob's mom, Lillian and sister Pat visit Bob on set.

CHINA DOLL

Johnny Desmond (l) and Bob from a scene in *China Doll*.
The movie was produced by John Wayne's Batjac Productions.

Left: Bob had the starring role as
Theseus in United Artist's *The
Minotaur*. (Notice the curly hair!)

Right: on the set of *The
Minotaur* with co-star Rosanna
Schiafino. The film was made in
Rome, Italy.

THE MINOTAUR

THE TROUBLESHOOTERS

In 1959 and '60, Bob co-starred with Keenan Wynne in the NBC-TV series *The Troubleshooters*, which aired on the network Friday nights at 8 p.m. "The hardest part in the work of movie making," Bob said, "was the waiting. I can sure vouch for actors who say making movies is hard work. You are on the set from dawn (and many times before) to dusk (and many times after). The waiting can be murder." However, Bob enjoyed making the 26 episodes of *The Troubleshooters* with his good friend. "Keenan was great to work with and he taught me a lot," Bob said. "He was a terrific actor."

Top left: Bob poses for a national magazine ad for Fortrel Fabrics. Bob did many print, television and radio ads for the likes of Vitalis hair products, Days slacks, General Electric, Iveco Trucks and others.

Bottom Left: The "well educated, socially polished, soft spoken" Frank Dugen, played by Bob Mathias on *The Troubleshooters*.

"We were proud to serve our country and that is what we were supposed to do."

Bob Mathias,
upon being sworn into the Marine Corps.

Bob served two and a half years active duty as an officer in the Marine Corps and was discharged in 1956. After he got out of the service, Bob did some touring for the U.S. State Department and also for the United States Olympic Committee, which he is still active with today. On occasion Bob traveled with other athletes and some of the touring was done alone. He developed a keen interest in foreign policy and observing how the various governments conducted their programs. "I was very fortunate to be able to meet with many officials from the various countries and cities," Bob said, "and I also had good contact with the citizens during my demonstrations of the decathlon."

Bob meets with President Eisenhower in California.

Lt. Bob Mathias, U.S. Marines

There were the many tours he went on, both in competitive track meets (along with other prime U.S. athletes) and the special personal tours he went on all over the globe representing the American people through the U.S. State Department or as a personal representative of President Eisenhower. Oftentimes Bob would make an appearance in a country where up to 40,000 people would turn out just to see this great athlete demonstrate his gifts and to hear him speak.

To say that Bob Mathias was in demand in the 1950s would be putting it way too lightly.

TRAVELIN' MAN

BOB AS GOODWILL AMBASSADOR

Many people around the world had looked forward to seeing Bob go for an unheard-of third Olympic gold medal, but it just wasn't to be.

When Bob was released from active duty in the Marine Corps, he thought about the possibility of competing in the 1956 Olympic Games in Melbourne, Australia. He was in great shape and had won his last decathlon (an all-service decathlon) overwhelmingly. Knowing that he had been declared a professional by Avery Brundage and the International Olympic Committee because of the money he had been paid to do *The Bob Mathias Story*, Bob wrote a letter to Dan Ferris, the AAU president, to see if it would be possible to gain back his amateur status. "Dan told me 20 different things I would have to do to be eligible for the Olympics again," Bob said, "including giving back all the money I'd made from the movie. Since I'd already spent it, that would have been tough. I had a family to raise and I didn't want to have my folks support me, so I realized what the reality was and got on with life. Looking back, in this day and age of the incredible money the "amateur" athletes are paid, almost makes Bob's situation of ineligibility seem outrageous, but that was the situation and he accepted it. Not bitterly, Bob says, "I was still only 25, I was at my peak, still growing as an athlete. It would have been fun." Most experts agree he would have won going away.

(cont. on p. 58)

Olympic legend Jesse Owens and Bob at one of their many appearances together.

England

Hawaii

Egypt

China

Belgian Congo

WELL, IT'S PAKISTAN BUT WHERE'S BOB?

(cont. from p. 56)

Bob Mathias retired from decathlon competition, with a record of 11-0, the only decathlete to ever retire undefeated.

Bob would go to the Games in 1956, not as a competitor, but as a personal representative of President Eisenhower. Milt Campbell, who was a silver medalist behind Bob in the Helsinki games, wound up winning the gold medal in the '56 Games in Melbourne. Campbell's U.S.A. teammate, Rafer Johnson, won the silver medal. Johnson, also from the San Joaquin Valley, a few miles from where Mathias was raised, would also go on the win the gold in 1960. Mathias, Campbell and Johnson, as so many of the Olympic decathletes have, still remain good friends today.

Bob's goodwill tours for the U.S. State Department and entities such as the Amateur Athletic Union (AAU), and the United States Olympic Committee were plentiful. He was a main attraction and drew huge crowds; sometimes as many as 40,000 people would turn out to hear Bob speak or watch a demonstration of his athletic ability, or just to catch a glimpse of one of the 20th century's true heroes. He organized and encouraged fitness, sports and youth programs in America, Europe, Asia, Africa and Latin America.

New York

Africa

Iran

Pakistan

China

A MATHIAS MEMORY

There has always been a love affair between Bob Mathias and the people of Tulare, California. Both sides of that affair always brought great things to the table. Bob Mathias brought the international acclaim of his Olympic accomplishments and Tulare answered with its great support of their hometown hero with parades and adulation. Mathias was featured in a Hollywood movie about his life and Tulare answered with great excitement and cooperation with the film's producers when parts of the movie were shot on location in "Mathiasville" (Tulare). Respect and honor for Bob brought three National Decathlon Championship meets to town and Tulare (and the Valley) responded by making all three enormously successful sellouts. (Bob responded again by winning all three times!) The list goes on and on. Bob served four terms in the House of Representatives and Tulare came up with a first-rate museum exhibit that still thrills the home folk and brings visitors from all over to Tulare. Then there have been the dinners and special events that honored Bob and other favorite sons and daughters of Tulare and their accomplishments.

One of those special events took place in early November of 1977, and it still stands very close to the heart of Bob Mathias. On November 9, 1977, a dinner was held in the Sim Iness gymnasium on the campus of Tulare Western High School. The dinner was in honor of the high school football stadium being renamed Bob Mathias Stadium the following night during pregame ceremonies of the Tulare Western and Tulare Union football game. Both the dinner and the game were sold out for the historic occasion. Bob's parents, Dr. Charlie and Lillian, along with brothers Dr. Eugene, James and sister Patricia were all on hand, along with his high school coaches Virgil Jackson and Ernie Lambrecht and many friends and teammates from his days in Tulare. At this time, Bob was serving as director of the United States Olympic Training Center at Colorado Springs, Colorado. It was a great occasion for him to get back home for a visit and to see everyone. Rafer Johnson, Bob's good friend from Kingsburg, California, just 20 miles north said, "I'm always honored to be in a place where people honor great champions." The former Olympic decathlon champion, who broke Bob's world decathlon record while winning the gold medal at the Games in Rome in 1960, continued, "Bob Mathias is a champion on and off the field of competition. It's really something that his town would call him back after nearly 30 years. It's something that you feel that strongly about him. People in Tulare should be congratulated for what Bob Mathias has accomplished. Coming from a small town myself, I know how important its support can be."

And that's how the evening went. Lots of love passed around. Bob was praised by track legend Cornelius "Dutch" Warmerdam (former world record holder in the pole vault), who said, "Mathias was the best of his era, and if he were competing today, he'd still be the best." Bob's high school buddy and teammate and fellow 1952 Olympic gold medal winner (in the discus), Sim Iness, told of some great times the two friends had growing up in Tulare. "I still think of Bob as one of the good ole' boys," Sim said laughing. "We enjoyed hillbilly singing and playing guitar and just hanging around with friends." Iness also spoke of the many teams that the two had played on and Sim gave credit to Bob, saying, "Bob Mathias was always an inspiration to me."

After the speeches and presentations, including film clips from Bob's decathlon and football careers, as well as film clips of the enthusiastic greetings he received upon his returns home were shown, Bob graciously thanked his beloved hometown once again for the special occasion. "The best and fondest memories I have are from old Tulare Stadium and I am so proud and grateful that it is being renamed for me."

The next night, a capacity crowd turned out for the dedication ceremonies and saw a great high school football game between two rivals. Bob watched the first half of the game on the Tulare Union side, and then was escorted to the Tulare Western side of the field for the second half. Also that night, the crowd was able to see for the first time the brand new all-weather track, which made Bob Mathias Stadium one of the most modern track and field facilities in the Valley.

C.T.

1966

OUR MAN IN WASHINGTON

On November 8, 1966, Bob Mathias was elected to serve in the 90th Congress. He would be representing the people of California's 18th Congressional District in the U.S. House of Representatives. Bob was re-elected to serve in the 91st, 92nd and 93rd Congresses as well. Those years, 1967 to 1975, were turbulent years in American history. "Vietnam changed us," Bob said. "People did not believe that they were doing something for their country. Many felt it was just dying in a foreign land. It was very complicated and caused division. I think some of that lasts today."

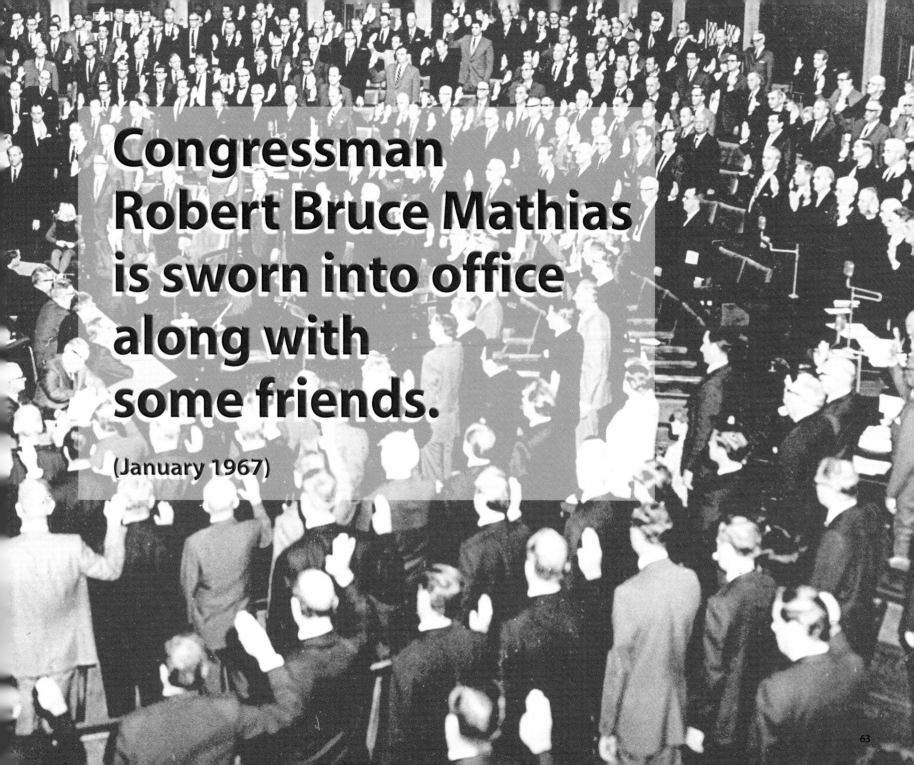

Congressman Robert Bruce Mathias is sworn into office along with some friends.

(January 1967)

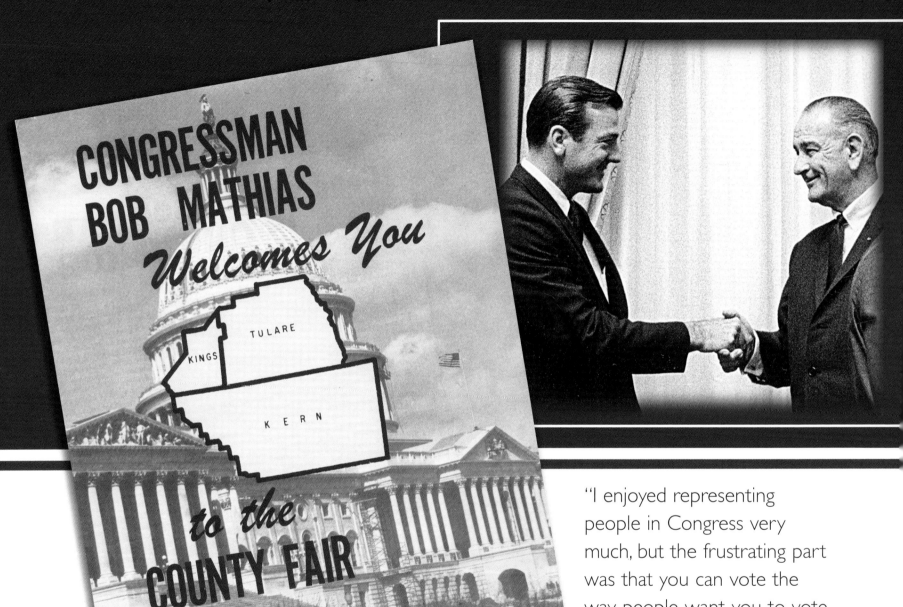

"I enjoyed representing people in Congress very much, but the frustrating part was that you can vote the way people want you to vote 99 times out of a hundred, and if they don't like that

100th vote, that's the one they never forget. You just have to deal with the fact that you can't please everybody and you just do the very best you can." After four terms in Congress and a defeat in the 1974 election, Bob looked to other bridges to cross.

After his years in Washington, Bob served as director of the U.S. Olympic Training Center in Colorado Springs. In his eight years as director he helped build it into the world class training facility it still is today. Thousands of athletes have trained at the center on their way to representing the United States around the world. Just like the London Olympics in 1948 was "just another track meet" to Bob, the way he looked at the USOTC was another way to put his talents to great use.

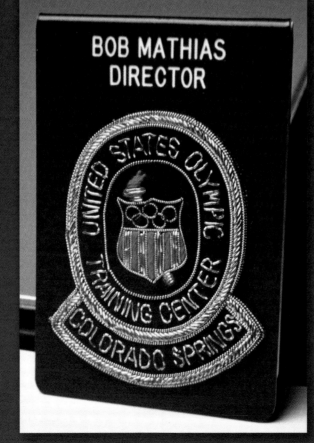

Admiral Elmo "Bud" Zumwalt was happy to see Bob come to Washington. And sorry to see him go. "Bob was a great sports hero and a true American hero. He is still a hero around the globe. I think he could have been president of the United States. He was that popular and loved. Intelligent too."

Beach Boy Bruce Johnson meets a living legend.

Bob, as executive director of the National Fitness Foundation, meets with Peter Ueberroth and John Wooden.

If a visitor assumed there would be medals and other awards for sports activities hanging on the walls of the Mathias home in Fresno, California, that visitor would be correct, although the Olympic gold medals and the bulk of the trophies and such are housed in the Tulare Museum, 50 miles to the south. If one assumed that those athletic awards at home had the name of the great Olympic decathlete on them, the visitor would only be partially correct. That's because many of the awards have the name "Gwen" on them. Gwen Mathias, Bob's accomplished and supportive wife of more than 20 years, is quite an athlete in her own right. She was an all-conference player on her high school basketball team back in Forest City, Arkansas. Gwen Haven was an all-around athlete, participating in volleyball, swimming and tennis (where she also excelled), but her love was basketball.

BOB AND GWEN
Today

Bob and Gwen carry a torch for each other. Here they carry an Olympic torch for all of us en route to the 1984 Games.

Whenever possible, Gwen accompanies Bob on his many appearance trips. Here they are in New York for the premiere of Disney's *Hercules* and a guest appearance on ABC's *Good Morning America.*

Bob and Gwen Mathias have many interests that both love. They like to travel and visit friends, go camping, and entertain at their place near Kings Canyon National Park. They both love to swim and do so everyday from May to October, either at their home in Fresno or up at the lake by their mountain home. When Bob sold the Bob Mathias Camp (a youth camp that Bob ran for 17 years) a number of years ago, he held on to some acres and developed them for their getaway time. Bob and Gwen have a mobile home there and there is a very homey campfire area, which gets plenty of use on weekends. Friends often join them for campouts, horseshoes, storytelling and singing around the campfire, and walks through the woods.

Bob and Gwen on the road. That's their camper in the background.

UNITED STATES OLYMPIC DECATHLON CHAMPIONS
OF THE
LAST HALF-CENTURY

Bob Mathias, 1948 and 1952

Bruce Jenner, 1976

Rafer Johnson, 1960

Bill Toomey, 1968

Milt Campbell, 1956

(clockwise, from bottom left)

Dan O'Brien, 1996 (not pictured)

Look at how much Bob improved in the just over four years of competition in his decathlon career. His first decathlon was in the Pasadena Games, held at the Los Angeles Coliseum in 1948 when Bob was 17 and less than two months from winning the Olympics that year. Comparing the times and lengths between that competition with Bob's results in the 1952 Games in Helsinki, quite a story is told.

	PASADENA (1948)	**HELSINKI (1952)**
100 meters	11.1 seconds	10.9 seconds
Long jump	21 feet, 4 and 1/2 in.	22 feet, 10 and 3/4 inches
16-lb. shot put	43 feet, 1 inch	50 feet, 2 and 5/8 inches
High jump	5 feet, 10 inches	6 feet, 2 and 3/4 inches
400 meters	52.1 seconds	50.2 seconds
110-meter high hurdles	15.7 seconds	14.7 seconds
Discus	140 feet, 1/8 inch	153 feet, 10 inches
Pole vault	11 feet, 9 inches	13 feet, 1 and 1/2 inches
Javelin	175 feet, 4 and 5/8 in.	194 feet, 3 and 1/8 in.
1,500 meters	4 minutes, 59.2 sec.	4 minutes, 50.8 seconds

FROM THOSE WHO KNOW HIM...

When Bob retired from decathlon competition, he did so with an undefeated record. Dr. Frank Zarnowski, recognized decathlon expert, speaks of that accomplishment: "Even Daley Thompson (1980 and 1984 Olympic champ) and Dan O'Brien (1996 Olympic champ) lose once in a while. In five years of competition and 11 meets, Bob never lost. He was the best of his era, and he proved it by destroying all his competitors," Zarnowski said. "He is one of the three greats in the history of the sport who never lost, but the other two, Jim Thorpe and Glenn Morris, had careers of only one and three meets."

70th
Bob Mathias - Fresno Relays

Ratcliffe Stadium

50 years ago, Bob Mathias won his first gold medal in the decathlon at the 1948 Olympics in London.

This year, Fresno State junior Melissa Price became the first-ever NCAA women's pole vault champion.

April 2-4, 1998

When Bob won the Best Prep Athlete trophy in 1947 and 1948 at the West Coast Relays, little did he know that the prestigious meet would one day be named in his honor. The Bob Mathias-Fresno Relays meet, hosted by California State University, Fresno, is still one of the premier events in track on the West Coast.

"I first met Bob at the Southern Pacific AAU Decathlon Championships at the Los Angeles Coliseum. I liked him from the beginning. He was friendly and unassuming. A very tall young guy, lean and looking most impressive in his red satin warm-ups with TULARE emblazoned across the front. He was mature, but he looked so young. But of course, he **was** young.

"He never got rattled or distracted in that first decathlon. I saw him display that quality many times in competition in the years to come."

Floyd Simmons,
Olympic decathlon
bronze medalist,
1948 and 1952

"My inspiration was Bob Mathias."

Sim Iness, 1993 (On his winning the gold medal in the discus at the 1952 Games)

"A true American hero, Bob Mathias was always a great representative of the United States as not only a great athlete but as a great ambassador."

Charlton Heston, actor

———————————————

"Bob was always an inspiration for me. His competitiveness, his strength, and his work ethic was the stuff that legends are made of."

Bruce Jenner, Olympic decathlon champion, 1976

———————————————

"Bob's winning the decathlon gold medal at the age of 17 has got to be one of the greatest athletic accomplishments of all time. And that was just the beginning of a legendary career!"

Bob Costas, sports broadcaster and commentator

"I think it was a shame that he didn't compete in the 1956 Games. He would have won. I know Bob was a country kid, but he was surely a hero to a lot of city kids, like me, as well. Brooklyn loved him!"

Larry King, CNN host of Larry King Live

"It was a shame what was decided about Mathias' amateur standing in 1956. I think Bob was robbed but I think the world was robbed more! Mathias was in his prime and would have won again."

Pat Tobin, Chicago TV personality

"To me, he's a real champion, not only because of what he did, but because he is a real human being."

Pat McCormick, winner of two gold medals in diving, 1952 and 1956

FROM THOSE WHO KNOW HIM ...

"I was with the Philadelphia A's in 1948, and we all thought it was fantastic what Bob did that summer in London. We talked about it every day. Just amazing."

Gus Zernial, former American League home run champ

"Bob Mathias did some great things for this Valley (the San Joaquin Valley). I'd love to vote for him again right now."

Earl Smittcamp
Founder, Wawona Farms

"Bob is a terrific help to us and never turns us down in helping our programs and athletes. He especially is an inspiration to our athletes in terms of encouragement and personal counseling."

Harry Marra, U.S. national decathlon team coach

"Bob handled it all so well. He was humble and kind to everyone. The kids just idolized him. It was amazing."

Tom Hennion, editor of the Tulare Advance Register in 1948

———————————

"He's always been good to me. He always thinks about sending a card from his travels. I've been very fortunate to have a brother that likes me, and takes care of me and doesn't neglect me. I feel the same about him, Gene and Pat."

Jim Mathias

———————————

"Bob Mathias is our greatest athlete, ever."

Jack Kemp, former U.S. congressman and quarterback, Buffalo Bills

FROM THOSE WHO KNOW HIM ...

"I think the key to Bob's success was his uncanny ability to relax in any situation. Not many people could actually fall asleep before an event, but Bob could. He just didn't let things bug him."

Bruce Farris, sportswriter, **The Fresno Bee**

_____

"Bob truly became an icon for the ideals I wanted to represent as an athlete."

Dave Johnson, former U.S.A. decathlon champ

_____

"Bob Mathias is the last 'real Olympian.' He is a role model of what athletes used to be."

Bill Toomey,
Olympic decathlon champion, 1968

"I grew up on a small farm village near Bob's hometown of Tulare. I was so proud and inspired that a person from the Central Valley could influence the world with his athletic gifts. Bob made dreams possible for all us country kids."

Kerry Yo Nakagawa,
Founder of the Diamonds in the Rough Japanese-Americans in Baseball,
International Exhibit

"When I was in sixth grade, my teacher (Tom Ramage) took some of us kids up to the Bob Mathias Camp during the winter as a special weekend treat to pay back the honor students. The highlight of the weekend was that we were going to get to meet Bob Mathias. I couldn't wait. We even got to eat dinner at his house. I remember so well what a down-to-earth person he was. It was an inspiring experience. In the excitement, I forgot to bring my camera so I didn't get a picture and I was so shook up that I forgot to get his autograph, but I NEVER forgot the thrill."

Jeral Richardson, police officer, the first athlete ever to high
jump seven feet at Fresno City College and
California State University, Fresno

"Bob has been a winner on and off the field of play. He is probably the most underrated athlete of the century."

Peter Ueberroth, former commissioner of
Major League Baseball

"Growing up in Tulare was really wonderful. We had it all. There was a great bunch of kids to run around with and the reason for that was that there was a great bunch of parents around. The group we grew up with, well, most of the parents would be at every event if they could. They wouldn't be meddling and interfering, but they were positive, and when one of us was messing up in school or whatever, because of that tight-knit involvement among the parents, we got straightened out real quick."

Bob Hoegh, Mathias buddy and teammate

When Bob was in the House of Representatives, he was the first to introduce the Amateur Sports Act. The bill, which finally passed in 1978, was designed to let people from national governing bodies for specific sports, govern themselves. It eliminated the Amateur Athletic Union (A.A.U.) which oversaw the governing of all amateur sports. The legislation allowed each sport to concentrate on its own and it gave the U.S. Olympic Committee more power to do things. For example, after the United States had a relatively poor showing in the 1976 Games in Montreal, the U.S.O.C. realized that Russia and East Germany pretty much had a leg up on the rest of the world teams by holding sports camps where athletes could train for the Olympics. In 1977, the committee decided to do something to level the playing field. They opened the United States Olympic Training Center in Colorado Springs. The site was an abandoned air force base that needed a lot of work. They began a search for a very special director to get the project in motion. The U.S.O.C. didn't have to look far. Who better than one of the greatest Olympic athletes of all time and one who had earlier built and run the Bob Mathias Sierra Camp for Boys and Girls, for 16 years, in California? Bob gladly accepted the challenge. "My job was to refurbish the old and build the new facilities," Bob said. "It was great. It was like I was in the hotel business, then the restaurant business, the training business, and so on.

The job was varied and so it kept you busy because there was so much to do, but wow, it sure was interesting! And I just loved living in Colorado."

Bob started to work in June and by December, athletes from all over the country began to arrive. "It was a wonderful atmosphere," Bob remembers. "I loved to see the great young people come in and get the training they needed. Over the years, hundreds of different athletes from a hundred different cities, getting coached by the best coaches. It gave so many more people the opportunity to make the U.S. team and the concept obviously has helped the U.S. Olympic effort." Bob served as the director of the U.S.O.T.C. for eight years. He still likes to go back, "At least once a year," to visit with friends and enjoy the always improving facility. His daughter, Megan, still lives in Colorado Springs. One year after Bob began to build the center in Colorado Springs, the U.S.O.C. moved their offices from New York City to Colorado Springs and they are still there today.

Maybe some day they'll name the center after Bob, too! In any case, it stands as a monument to his hard work and vision. Bob never forgot his roots. He exploded onto the world scene in the 1948 Olympics. He will forever promote the ideals of Olympic competition.

C.T.

FROM THOSE WHO KNOW HIM ...

Question: Would Bob Mathias have won the Olympic decathlon gold had he been allowed to compete in the 1956 Games in Melbourne, Australia?

Answers: "No doubt in my mind whatsoever. Bob would have won."

Dr. Sammy Lee, weightlifting gold medalist, 1948 and 1952

"I'm sure of it."

Bill Toomey, decathlon gold medal winner, 1968

"The Mathias family was always very supportive of each other and very nice people basically. Plus they all had a great sense of humor."

Tom Hennion, former editor, Tulare Advance Register

"Bob was so mentally tough, so physically strong, and a keen competitor. I can't even get on the same page as Bob Mathias on toughness. It's very few people who can face each varied event, for ten events, and stay so much on top of that event, with such proficiency, confidence and performance — all in one package. It's just incredibly tough to do. And to think of a 17-year-old to do that and then come back four years later and do it again, well, that's just got to be one of the greatest feats of all time."

Payton Jordan, former track coach at Occidental and
Stanford University

"I was out to sea when Bob won in 1948, and when I heard about it I was thrilled. Everyone on the ship was. I was so proud of Bob and of Tulare."

Admiral Elmo "Bud" Zumwalt

―――――――――――

"I still consider Mathias in London the most exciting story I ever covered, certainly the biggest sports story I ever wrote."

Paul Zimmerman, sports editor, 1939 to 1968
The Los Angeles Times

―――――――――――

"An upbeat, inspiring story about an American icon. Bob's life will forever set a standard of excellence."

Dan Patrick, ESPN SportsCenter

Bob endorsed many products and services over the years but always turned down commercials for beer and cigarettes. He did do promotions for insurance companies, Vitalis hair care products, and others, but he was never on the cover of the Wheaties box, although many people think he was. Oftentimes people say to him that they remember him on the Wheaties box, but no, he tells them, that was Bob Richards, the Olympic gold medal winner in the pole vault at the 1952 Games and good friend of Bob's. The irony is that Bob Mathias was asked to do a Wheaties box photo shoot, but he was on tour in Europe and Africa and couldn't come back to the states in time to do it.

From Those Who Know Him ...

"Bob and I grew up in the same area. I'm from just about 20 miles north of Tulare in the little town of Kingsburg. In 1952, my coach said 'You know, there is a great athlete down in Tulare (we knew about Bob after his winning the 1948 Olympics), and they are holding an Olympic trial meet in Tulare. Let's go and see this guy.' I've always looked up to Bob Mathias and the fact I've been able to accomplish a little bit in the decathlon and track and field Olympic competition — I owe a lot of it to Bob because he did inspire all of us young people."

Rafer Johnson,
Olympic decathlon champion, 1960

"I join Bob's many friends and colleagues in expressing my sincere congratulations and admiration on the celebration of the 50th anniversary of such a great achievement at the early age of 17 and every continuing successful accomplishment since that original important feat."

King Hussein, Amman, Jordan, remembering Bob in 1998

"Bob and I were always good friends. We each knew what the other was going through with all the sort of 'fame and glory' and all that. Heck, we both had our pictures on the cover of *TIME* magazine for heaven's sake. It was all a lot of fun but I think we didn't take it for anything else or made much of a deal over it. We just had some great times."

Parry O'Brien,
Olympic Hall of Famer

"Last week Tulare, California, was probably the only city in the U.S. where an 8-year-old youngster would rather get a discus for a Christmas present than a baseball bat."

LIFE *magazine article, July 11, 1949*

Bob Mathias and Rafer Johnson, two Olympic decathlon champions, raised just 20 miles apart.

Bob and Sim, the greats of Tulare.

"Who would have thought that I would ever go to college. My big ambition was to be the tallest peach-picker in Tulare County, and if it hadn't been for Coach Jackson and some other wonderful teachers, that might have been just what happened."

*Sim Iness, Olympic champion, 1952,
teacher and football coach*

───────────────────

"Bob was certainly an inspiration to a generation of American athletes. When youngsters saw what this amazing young athlete did in the eyes of the world, and who he was, he brought a great deal of interest to track and field."

*Al Oerter,
four-time Olympic gold medalist*

"I was always (and still am) amazed at what Bob did in the Olympics and other sports. His story was one of a real hero and a good role model to look up to."

Bill Bradley, former U.S. Senator,
Olympic gold medal winner, 1964
NBA all-star

"I've often wondered, as all of us do, what would happen if the past Olympic decathlon medalists were called to compete against each other. In this thought we are all perfectly trained to correlate to the year this competition holds. This would mean no athlete would have an advantage of training in the later years. No prior or lack of athletic knowledge would be allowed. The only item each individual could take with him is his spirit. His reason why he wants to be the best. A most glorious fight it would be. One that only God could fully appreciate. In the end a boy named Bob Mathias would stand above us all, and would still remain unchanged as a true representation of the Olympic spirit."

Dave Johnson,
four-time U.S.A. champion decathlete,
bronze medalist in 1992 Olympics

"How could I get to know him?
Hell, all I saw was his back!"

Dennis Weaver,
Hollywood actor and former decathlete,
who finished sixth behind Bob at the Olympic
Trials in 1948

"It, of course, is a real thrill to meet someone who you idolized for many years. Bob was a great inspiration to me and I always wanted to be like him. When I met him, he was friendly and he made it so easy. What a great guy."

Bruce Jenner,
decathlon gold medal winner in 1976

"Bob Mathias was always willing to give back. He has been a champion on so many fields in America and around the world. He has traveled the long miles in pursuit of promoting good feelings and harmony. A truly great inspiration to our young people for generations."

Gerald Ford,
former United States President

"The major thing with Bob is that he has always stayed the same. He never changed. He is still the same sincere, genuine person, totally unaffected by what has happened in his life. He's a great guy."

Gwen Mathias

QUESTIONS AND ANSWERS

WITH BOB MATHIAS

Q What was it like to be world famous at age 17?

A Well, when I won the gold medal in '48, I really didn't think much more of it than just winning another track meet. I knew it was good and people were sure nice to me but I guess I didn't realize what was going on so much. Stopping at the White House to see President Truman was great and all that sort of thing (the parade in San Francisco, etc.), but when I got back home and saw all my high school buddies, well, it wasn't long before things got back to normal. I'm sure today it would be a much bigger deal. I did get asked to a lot of banquets and things like that and it was wonderful for me because I got to meet all those famous athletes like Jim Thorpe, Joe DiMaggio, Glenn Morris and on and on ... so that was pretty great.

Q What would you think of a 17-year-old doing what you did then, today?

A Well, of course, things change. When I did it, there were no professional athletes in track. So you really did it for the fun of it and for the joy of competition. Nowadays track guys can get a lot of money, even though they still call them amateurs, from endorsements, appearances and the like so it would be much more difficult today because it would add so much more pressure to an already rigid training schedule. You have the element of working with agents, doing commercials and all that part of it versus just only thinking about your competition. That has to be tough. So much of competition is focusing on what you are doing.

Q What do you tell youngsters today about getting focused and setting goals?

A I like to tell about reading a story about Glenn Morris, the gold medal winner in the 1936 Games in Berlin, and then-world record holder in the decathlon. A year or so after I won in 1948, I had said that I was very grateful for having competed in the Games and winning the gold, but I wasn't going to compete again in the 1952 Games in Helsinki. I was going to be happy playing football and taking pre-Med courses at Stanford. Then one day I read this article about Glenn and what he did in '36 and I saw that he did 11.0 in the hundred and I said "I'd like to do 10.9," and then as I went through the 10 events and his times and measures, I thought, "You know, if I really worked hard, I think I could beat Glenn Morris' scores." All of a sudden, I had a goal for the first time in my life, and that was not to win the Olympics in '52, not to break the world record or any lofty goals like that, but simply to beat the marks of a guy named Glenn Morris. So that's what I did, working on each event with the goal in mind of beating one man's marks, just one day at a time and by the time I did manage to do that I was in great shape and ready to take on the next goal which was another Olympics. And then I set my sights on that. Staying focused one step at a time.

Q What do you think of the concept of athletes as role models?

A I think it's a good concept. When I grew up, most of the guys I knew as well-known athletes were also good citizens. Basically just good guys and gals that loved the sport, played it well, and were good role models to youngsters. There was, of course, always going to be a few who didn't care much, but for the most part, that's the way it was and I think today probably 80% of the athletes in the public eye are honorable people and good role models. But that other 20%, well, they just make it pretty ugly. I wish the owners just wouldn't hire them but I guess they feel they have to. Unfortunately, it all seems to be about winning and publicity one way or another. The money they pay out now is just ridiculous for some people who shouldn't be playing.

A Mathias gathering. That's Dr. Charlie and Lillian seated. Standing (l to r) Pat, Jim, Bob, Gene and Pricilla (Gene's wife).

Q What was meaningful to you about your movie career?

A It was a great experience, very interesting. I learned all about Hollywood. I met some very talented people as actors, producers, directors and I got to see how the movies are made. I had some great friends there like Keenan Wynne, John Wayne and many other hard working and talented people. I was truly amazed at the talent that these people had in putting the movies and television shows together. I had no idea what it took, so it was fun to see and I felt lucky to get to be a part of it for a while.

Q Mr. Congressman! How do you look back on your time in Washington?

A Well I liked it, no, I loved it. I loved mainly working with constituents trying to solve any problems they might have. Veterans, small business administration, farmers in the district and so forth. I felt you could accomplish something working one-on-one, working to solve problems with some agencies of the federal government. That was interesting to me. Sometimes it was boring in committee, listening to things (day after day after day on the same subject) even though you pretty much know how the vote is going to go. That can make it pretty tedious work. It's not as romantic as one might think ... lots of long hours, a great deal of traveling from Washington to home (California), etc. In order to serve your constituents well, you have to listen to what their needs are and I spent a lot of time doing that.

Q Oftentimes we see politicians in Washington really getting after each other in debate yet they almost seem like friends when they are not at work, so to speak. Is that the way it is?

A Well, that's true. I had a lot of friends on the other side of the aisle and you knew that they would vote exactly to the opposite of you. Completely opposite in our views, but personally, oftentimes you were friends ... you'd have dinner with them or go on trips and so forth, but in voting you would mostly just disagree. It would work the same way in them trying to help you get defeated.

Well, you can't take it personally, that's just the way politics are. I mean if someone would criticize you personally on the floor, or tell a lie personally, well, you would take offense, but if someone stands there and says that, "Bob voted a certain way and I think he's wrong," well, that's just how it works.

It's vicious today, they will do anything, no holds barred, and I think that's a main reason why they are having the trouble they are.

Q Would you run for political office today?

A No. I was happy and honored to serve four terms and I enjoyed the experience, but today there is a lot of ruthlessness and I don't think I would like to be there. I hope they can get it straightened out. Sometimes you wonder why anyone would want to run for Congress.

Q   What do you think is wrong in Washington today?

A   I think that members are spending too much time raising campaign funds. In-kind contributions are way, way up and candidates and incumbents will do anything for it. Raising money for your campaign is a necessary evil but legislators are spending more and more time at it, which is not good. They should be spending more time on their legislation.

Q   Do you believe in term limits?

A   I certainly do. I'd say eight years for a representative and perhaps two terms (12 years) for a senator. After that people become beholding to the people that give them the money. They tend to vote not the way their constituents want them to, but more to where the money comes from — the lobby groups, the special interest groups, labor unions, business or whatever it is.

This discus was once thrown by Bob. It is on display at the Tulare Historical Museum.

Q How can we get big money out of politics?

A It's a tough question because these are the people making the laws and many of them don't want to change the laws. It's too good for them the way it is. It's like with term limits. Many congressmen and senators don't want to change the law because they know they have it too good. They make great money now, they have no expenses, they have one heck of a good job. But I think it would be good to get fresh young blood in office, people that aren't tied to special interests and lobby groups. In years to come, I hope somebody has guts enough to stop it because it's not good.

Q Is there any envy on your part about the money that the athletes (Olympians) of today are getting?

A No, no envy whatsoever. I've joked that I was born too soon, you know, that if I was born 20 years later I would have made some money, but no, I have been fortunate to have been able to make some money in other areas in my life, just not in sports.

Q Do you think you have a special gift?

A Well, I think you are just born with some God-given talents. For some it might be physical, maybe others mental ... you can amplify it by training hard and having good coaches and working hard, but it is something that you are born with. I believe that I was very lucky to have a coach like Virgil Jackson who recognized things in me and guided me into the areas that best suited me. It's not something that you could do alone. You get a lot of help.

Q How did you handle the pressure that great competition brings, especially at such a young age?

A I always loved to compete. Pressure really didn't get to me much. I just always knew that I was going to do the best that I could and so I didn't let it bother me much. I was lucky about that. Inside me, I would get myself prepared to go out and do the very best I could. You might get a little nervous and get the butterflies a bit but for the most part I didn't worry about getting beat, I just knew that I was going to do the best I could. I suspected that my opponents would be doing the same, but I just tried to stay focused on doing the best that I could do.

Q You have often talked about Virgil Jackson, your football and track coach at Tulare High School. Was he the one who prepared you for the decathlon?

A Yes, he did. He had read about the decathlon in his research and suggested I give it a try. He told me about the Pasadena Games in Los Angeles that year and we thought it would be fun to try. Coach Jackson taught me how to do the 10 events and we practiced very hard. Sim (Innes) at the same time was being taught by Coach Jackson to throw the discus. Even though it was just a few months before the Olympics, none of us would even have the remotest thought about going all the way to the Olympics that year. (Bob eventually won the two golds in England and Finland, and Sim won the gold in the discus in Finland.)

———————————————

Q When you did make the Olympic team, how did the coaches handle you?

A Brutus Hamilton, the Olympics team coach in 1948, and his staff were great. They got us all together and told us that they weren't going to try to teach us anything, as they didn't want to have us change anything. Instead they just gave us training schedules to keep us in good shape to prepare for the Games. I kept on working on what Coach Jackson had taught me.

Q How were you, at 17, treated by the other athletes, in particular the decathletes Irving Mondschein (the world record holder) and Floyd Simmons?

A Oh, they were good guys ... They might have been a little skeptical at first, because of my age, but they were very supportive. We are still great friends after all these years and I always look forward to seeing Moon and Floyd.

Q What do you think would have happened if Virgil Jackson had not thought twice ... when reading about the decathlon, and never mentioned it to you back there in 1948?

A (Laughs) Well, I might have been a doctor. That was what I had been thinking about. I was in pre-Med my first year at Stanford but I changed because of the many obligations from the Olympic training and so forth.

Q Do you ever regret that?

A No, no. It did change my life and I would have liked being a doctor like my dad and brother but no, I feel very fortunate.

Q   Do you feel like you have led a charmed life?

A   I still feel that way, yes. Very lucky. When I read a poll like the ESPN Top 100 Athletes of the Century, I have to say, "Gee, did I really do that?" I was just having fun doing what I wanted to do. You have to wonder.

I'm very grateful.

A MATHIAS MEMORY

I have talked with a lot of people about Bob Mathias. I found out what a great person he is just by what everyone says about him. Never mind the incredible accomplishments: winning the Olympic gold medal in the decathlon at the age of 17 (a record that will NEVER be broken), then winning the gold again four years later in Helsinki, this time beating the second place finisher (Milt Campbell, who won the gold in the 1956 Games) by 912 points! How about the legendary USC-Stanford football game in 1951 in which a visit to the Rose Bowl was on the line. Bob's two fourth quarter touchdowns (including the 96-yard kickoff return against Frank Gifford and the favored Trojans) led Stanford to the upset victory in front of a packed Los Angeles Coliseum. The list goes on. What a competitor! What an athlete! To him, it's not so hard to figure out: "You have to work hard and stay with it, every day." Bob told me once holding up his thumb and index finger with a small gap between them: "The difference between winning and being an also-ran is that close! Work is the difference that can get you as high as you want to go."

Through it all, Bob never changed. It's the thing that amazes me the most. That he was always mainly just a nice, quiet, even shy, everyday person, with a genuine smile for everyone. Even though he was one of the greatest athletes of all time, he was and still is just a nice guy from a small town.

But truly an American hero.

C.T.

Bob's brother James was a track star at Occidental University.

TRULY ALL-AMERICAN

- OLYMPIC DECATHLON CHAMPION - 1948

- OLYMPIC DECATHLON CHAMPION - 1952

- SULLIVAN AWARD - 1948 (U.S. AMATEUR ATHLETE OF THE YEAR)

- TRACK & FIELD NEWS ATHLETE OF THE YEAR - 1948

- LED STANFORD TO 1952 ROSE BOWL

- ASSOCIATED PRESS ATHLETE OF THE YEAR - 1952

- HELMS ATHLETIC FOUNDATION TRACK & FIELD HALL OF FAME - 1953

- UNDEFEATED CAREER IN DECATHLON (11-0)

- U.S. CONGRESSMAN - 1967 to 1975

- BOB MATHIAS STADIUM DEDICATED AT TULARE HIGH SCHOOL - 1977

- DIRECTOR, U.S. OLYMPIC TRAINING CENTER - 1977 to 1985

- RANKED 76TH BEST ATHLETE OF THE 20TH CENTURY BY ESPN - 1999

- GOODWILL AMBASSADOR EXTRAORDINAIRE FOR THE U.S.A.

If you are ever traveling through Central California, Tulare is a great little town to visit. It is right off California State Highway 99. Tulare is about 45 minutes south of the connection with Highway 41 in Fresno that takes you right to Yosemite National Park, one of the most beautiful places in the world. Kings Canyon National Park is also close to Tulare and a wonderful place to visit. A real treat awaits you at the Tulare Museum. The museum is the home of the Bob Mathias Collection and features more than 1,000 items of interest from Bob's career. The gold medals, the Sullivan Award, wonderful photographs, the incredible collection of memorabilia from Bob's triumphs on the sports fields, as well as his movies, time in Washington, D.C., and his many travels around the world. Dr. Charlie and Lillian worked tirelessly over the years putting the items together to be shared with all. The museum also houses a section dedicated to Admiral Elmo "Bud" Zumwalt, another favorite son of Tulare. Sim Iness, General Maurie Preston and Bryan Allen as well as other famous Tulareans are featured.

The Tulare Historical Society and Museum, under the direction of Ellen Goreleck, is constantly adding new items to the Mathias and Zumwalt collections and also to the many pieces and displays of the history of the Tulare County area. You will be very pleasantly surprised, not only by the creative displays and the artifacts, but by the best Tulare product of all, the warm and friendly people you will meet there.

The Tulare City Historical Society
Tulare Historical Museum
444 W. Tulare Avenue
PO Box 248
Tulare, CA 93275

ABC-TV	5
Allied Artists	47, 48, 49
Associated Press	24, 25, 27, 40, 43, 44
Batjac Productions	50
Disney	70
Delores Iness	91
International Olympic Committee	16
Fritzie Jackson	29
Kiski Prep	31
NBC-TV	51
Randall Priester	3, 6, 14, 16, 17, 26, 29, 31, 34, 35, 39, 40, 42, 66, 74, 75, 94, 101
Stanford University	35, 36, 37, 38
Chris Terrence	66, 68
Tulare Advance - Register	15, 27, 32, 33, 44, 45, 62, 107
U.S. Marine Corps	53
United Artists	50

All other photos courtesy Mathias Family Collection